11/15(3)

Neymar

TO THE TOP!

2012 Wins the Ferenc Puskas Trophy, given by FIFA to the player who scores the best goal of the season.

2011 Wins his first international competition with Brazil, the South American U-20 Championship. He is the top scorer and most valuable player of the tournament.
Wins the São Paulo State Championship with Santos.
Santos wins the Copa Libertadores, the most important club competition in South America, and Neymar is voted MVP.
Wins the Bronze Ball (third best player) of the FIFA Club World Cup.

2010 Wins first title, the São Paulo state championship.
Wins the Brazil Cup, the second most important tournament of the Brazilian soccer schedule.
Debuts with the Brazilian national team against the U.S., and scores a goal in the 2-0 win.
Elected best young player and the second best forward in the Brazilian championship.

2009 Debuts as a professional with Santos against Oeste de Itápolis at São Paulo state championship.
Scores his first professional goal against Mogi Mirim during the São Paulo State Championship
Competes for Brazil in the under-17 World Championship. The team is eliminated in the first round.

2006 Considers a move to Real Madrid, but agrees to return to Santos.

2003 Join Santos as a youth player

1992 Born in Mogi das Cruzes, São Paulo.

Personal File

Name: Neymar da Silva Santos Júnior
Nicknames: Menino da Vila, Magrelo, Jóia
Birthplace: Mogi das Cruzes, SP
Nationality: Brazilian
Zodiac sign: Aquarius
Height: 5 feet 9 inches (1.74 m)
Twitter: @Njr92
Position: Forward
Preferred number: 11

ISBN-13: 978-1-4222-2648-3 (hc) — 978-1-4222-9189-4 (ebook)

Printing (last digit) 9 8 7 6 5 4 3 2 1
Printed and bound in the United States of America.
CPSIA Compliance Information: Batch #S2013. For further information, contact Mason Crest at 1-866-MCP-Book.

About the Author: Thiago Jorge Teixeira has worked as a sports journalist since 2004, when he began his career at Lance! magazine. Since 2005 he has worked at SporTV, the most watched sports channel in Brazil, where he is a director and producer. He co-wrote the book SporTV Olympic Almanac, and was one of the authors of the SporTV guide for the 2010 World Cup. It is common to see him at sporting activities throughout Brazil.

Photo credits: EFE/Leandro Amaral: 22; EFE/Harold Escalona: 17; EFE/Peter Foley: 14, 18; EFE/JuanJo Martin: 7; EFE/Kimimasa Mayama: 4; EFE/Sebastião Moreira: 10, 12, 20; EFE/Sandro Pereyra: 26; EFE/ Marcelo Sayao: 1, 23; PR Newswire: 25; Alexandru Cristian Ciobanu / Shutterstock.com: 2; Dalayo / Shutterstock.com: 16; Wikimedia: 24.

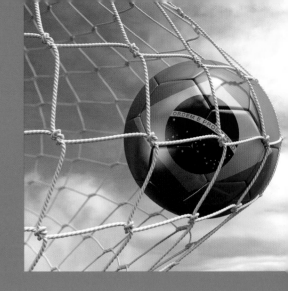

TABLE OF CONTENTS

Brazilian striker Neymar of Santos holds the bronze ball trophy while shaking hands with FC Barcelona's Lionel Messi (left), after Barca defeated Santos in the final of the Club World Cup in Japan, December 2011.

The Award-Winning Goal

ON THE NIGHT OF JULY 27, 2011, SANTOS WAS BEATING Flamengo 2-0 when, at the 25th minute, the Santos striker Neymar received the ball at the left side near midfield. With great skill, he dribbled between two defenders, passed the ball to a teammate, and ran forward to receive the ball back. After that, he left two defenders behind and fooled the goaltender with a spectacular move, passing the ball over his head to score. It was a magical moment, and Neymar was already smiling in celebration when the ball hit the net. It was a great goal.

In Brazil, a goal of this category is considered a "gol de placa" since the legendary Pelé won a plate at Maracana for the beauty of a goal he had scored against Fluminense. With his moves against Flamengo, Neymar inaugurated a new category: the award-winning goal.

A little more than six months after this goal was scored, on February 9, 2012, FIFA would recognize Neymar's talent by awarding him the Puskas Trophy. This is an award given to the player who scores the best goal of the year. The award was an affirmation for a boy who made the choice to play soccer in his home country, despite the interest of the major European clubs in hiring the player for their side.

"I was already happy to be here, competing with two great player for the trophy," Neymar said. "I don't know if I can make a better goal than that one. It is this goal that will be remembered in my career."

Mohawk Invasion

It is true that Brazil is the country of samba. But in the last two years, the most popular hairstyle among kids is the Mohawk, a classic of the punk-rock music movement of the late 1970s. This phenomenon has nothing to do with the music of bands like the Clash, Ramones, and Sex Pistols. The reason for this hairstyle's return to popularity goes by the name of Neymar da Silva Santos Júnior.

Neymar did not become the idol of a generation for no reason. During the first two years of his professional career, he has won major titles and has already scored more than 100 goals, many of them great ones. On the field the young player mesmerizes audiences with disconcerting movements, unthinkable passes, and a lot of charisma.

This charisma is a differential for Neymar, and it's almost as important as his football. He has an easy smile and an irreverence typical of the boy he still is. Neymar is friendly, and is always willing to meet fans for autographs and photos. He is currently being sought by many companies as an advertising spokesperson, as well as by European soccer clubs, which are always eager to import talented Brazilian players. Neymar has become a symbol of the renewal of the Brazilian national team after its World Cup disappointment in 2010. He is the greatest hope for the World Cup in Brazil 2014, and even won a beauty contest on the internet. In short, Neymar is the biggest hero of Brazilian football today.

Meteoric rise

Neymar was born in Mogi das Cruzes, a quiet town of almost 400,000 inhabitants in the Brazilian state of São Paulo. His father, also called Neymar, is a former football player. He was the first person to encourage Neymar to play soccer, when he was only nine years old. "I put pressure on him when he was nine, when I saw he had talent to become a great player," his father later said.

When Neymar was 10 years old, he left Mogi das Cruzes to play for the youth team at FC Santos, one of the most famous clubs in Brazil. There he quickly became a favorite of the coaches. From an early age Neymar was treated as a jewel. He was often compared to the great player Robinho, who had also trained as a youth

Neymar celebrates after scoring against Honduras during the London 2012 Olympic Games. He finished the Olympics with three goals, but Brazil lost in the final to Mexico.

with Santos and who was the club's biggest star at the time. Videos showing Neymar's skill with the ball were released by major television stations, and the young player began to receive a salary from the club.

In 2006, when he was 14 years old, Neymar was invited to try out with the Spanish club Real Madrid. However, according to his father, he was not happy in Spain. "I was offered an apartment, schools for the children—Neymar has a sister—and good money," his father recalled. "We were ready to sign, but after a week Neymar started getting depressed. He stopped eat-

ing right, because he missed rice and beans. That made me decide that it was better for him to return to Santos."

Neymar rise to fame did not lack obstacles. All the attention and pampering given to him by the club, as well as his salary, made some of his teammates jealous. "The hardest thing was jealousy," his father said. "This has always happened. Parents of other young players did not like him to have a high salary while their children were earning little."

"I saw a teammate once saying that Neymar thought he owned the team," says

Fast Fact

Even before his debut as a professional, Neymar was known to Santos fans. In 2008, he had played for the Santos youth team in the São Paulo Juniors Cup, an under-20 tournament. It's not a surprise that during the match against Oeste, the fans chanted his name, demanding to see Neymar play.

Wagner Ribeiro, the player's agent. He denied that Neymar had a big head.

Three years later, not long after turning 17, Neymar would make his professional debut for Santos. There were 21,198 people actually present at Pacaembu stadium in São Paulo for his debut, although that number may grow over the years. After all, many people may say that were present for Neymar's first professional game, even if it is not true.

The day was March 7, 2009, and the opponent was the small club Oeste de Itápolis. The match was for the São Paulo state championship. He entered the game at the 14th minute of the second half replacing the Colombian Mauricio Molina,

and helped Santos win by a score of 2-1. The following week, Neymar scored his first goal as a professional. It was the club's final score in a 3-0 victory over Mogi Mirim.

The rest, as they say, is history. In just two years, Neymar has won many individual titles. First, he was chosen the best young player of the São Paulo State Championship in 2009. The following year he was chosen the most valuable player of that tournament. In 2010 he was also chosen the MVP for the Brazilian National Championship, given by the Brazilian Football Confederation. In 2011 he repeated that, and won the "Bola de Ouro" (Golden Ball), a prestigious award given by the most popular soccer magazine in Brazil, *Placar*.

Neymar had such a great year that he ended up being named MVP of the Americas by the Uruguayan newspaper *El Pais*, and the best young player in the world by *World Soccer* magazine.

The list of titles won by Santos is also considerable for a 20 year old: São Paulo State Championship and Brazil Cup in 2010, and São Paulo State Championship and the Copa Libertadores—the most important soccer tournament in South America—in 2011.

A Star Is Born

"HE JUST APPEARED AND PEOPLE ALREADY COMPARE HIM with Pelé. I think he can be better than Pelé." Few people would dare to make such a statement about a young soccer player. Fewer still would give credit to such words. But it was Edson Arantes do Nascimento—the great Pelé himself—who said that Neymar, one day, might even surpass him. There can be no better compliment than to have the king of soccer compare a young player to himself.

And to think that in the previous year Vanderlei Luxemburgo, one of the country's most famous coaches, had relegated Neymar to the bench. Luxemburgo was worried about starting the young player too early, despite the good performances Neymar had when entering the team. His explanation was always the same: "It will take time before Neymar is ready. He is too thin and still can't take the hits."

Apparently only Luxemburgo had not seen the grace with which the young player flew over the grass. Against the brutality of his adversaries, Neymar used the unpredictability of his movements. It was not uncommon for opposing players to find only the wind when they moved to stop the young striker. The results spoke for themselves. In the 49 games Neymar played in 2009, he scored 14 goals and nine assists—even

Neymar competes in a championship game against the legendary Brazilian Ronaldo Nazario de Lima of Corinthians in March 2009.

though he was a substitute most of the time.

In 2009 Neymar would also know the first major disappointment of his career. He was chosen for the Brazilian under-17 team for the Youth World Cup tournament in Nigeria. He was one of the biggest stars on the team, along with midfielder Philippe Coutinho of Vasco da Gama. However, despite the hype, the team played very poorly and was eliminated in the first round.

Hero Dad

Despite the disappointment, Neymar did not become too depressed. This was most-

ly because of the support given by his father. A former football player, Neymar's dad knew how to manage the problems of early fame and gave his son support when it was needed. "We can help only to a certain point," Neymar's father explained. "This experience will make Neymar grow. We also learn from adversity. He now knows what is like to be disqualified before you are ready and to have to come back home disappointed."

Neymar's father is also his manager, and has guided his son's career with an iron hand. He helps with Neymar's contract negotiations, follows the photo and film crews that record his son's exploits, and often travels with the team. Neymar says that he is happy to receive all the support from his father. "I'm always learning from him," the young player says. "All advice is valuable."

Thanks to his father's advice, Neymar knew how to wait his turn. He behaved, accepted his time as a bench player, and overcame the trauma of failure with the under-17 national team. Aware of his promise, Santos assigned the player a special weight-lifting program to make him bigger and stronger. In 2010, Vanderlei Luxemburgo was let go as manager of Santos. With a new coach in place, Neymar would get his turn to be a starter.

Devastating Attack

As a coach, Dorival Júnior is known for helping young players to succeed. Hired to lead Santos for the 2010 season, Dorival found in Vila Belmiro the perfect environment for his type of work. Santos was a young and talented club, and two players were nearly ready to emerge as stars: Neymar and Paulo Henrique Ganso.

In a team sport like soccer, talent alone doesn't win every time. Chemistry on the field and friendship are also necessary to make a difference. These are qualities that Neymar and Ganso have to spare. They are almost the same age, and had been playing together in the youth division of Santos for years. Under the guidance of Dorival Júnior, they became the most reliable players for Santos. Along with Robinho, a star

Fast Fact

The comparison with Pelé is not the only one that Neymar has had to face. While emerging and making his name, the boy has been compared to Robinho, Ronaldo, and even Diego Maradona. *Olé*, the main Argentine sports newspaper, has referred to the young Santos striker as "Neymaradona."

player who returned to Santos in 2010 after six years playing in Europe and England, they created an attack that was the best in Brazilian soccer.

In the 2010 Brazil Cup, Neymar helped Santos destroy Naviraiense by an incredible 10-0 score. The traditional power Guarani was defeated 8 to 1. Overall, Santos scored 39 goals in 11 games. In 23 games for the São Paulo state championship, Santos scored 72 goals. This included games like a 9-1 victory over Ituano. Overall, in half a season, Santos scored 111 goals in 32 official matches. The best word to define their attack would be "unstoppable."

Off the field, Neymar and Paulo Henrique Ganso are also good friends. They spend time together and share hotel rooms when they are traveling. The two young players have very different backgrounds and personalities. Ganso is more relaxed, almost shy, while Neymar in private shows the same spontaneity and irrev-

Neymar fights for the ball with Alexandre Luiz Fernandes (Alê) of Santo André in a state championship game in May 2010.

erence that he exhibits on the soccer field with the ball at his feet.

The First Title

Despite the powerful attack of Santos in 2010, all the success would end in disappointment if the team did not win a championship. On May 2, 2010, Santos faced Santo André in the final game of the São Paulo state championship. Santos was a clear favorite. They had already won the first leg of the finals by a large-enough margin that they could even lose this game by one goal and still be crowned the champions. But the match started poorly for Santos. Santo André scored a goal in the first minute.

Neymar tied the score with a great goal in the 16th minute, carrying the ball past three players, including the goalkeeper, before scoring. Later, he would score a second goal, after exchanging passes with Robinho and Ganso. Ultimately, Santos lost the game, 3-2, but thanks to Neymar's goals they won the state championship anyway. "It was the best game of my life," said Neymar after the game.

Neymar's confidence in his football grew visibly. At times he had been criticized for excessive dribbling, but his success in the championship game gave him strength to keep his style. "Go ahead. We are champions. No one takes it from us," answered the boy.

His coach Dorival Júnior agreed, and praised the young player for his achievements on the field. "If we lost, it would be disrespect to football," the coach said.

At the moment that the São Paulo state championship ended, Neymar ceased to be a prospect and began to be a star. It was an exciting time—the 2010 World Cup would be starting in a few weeks. In Brazilian newspapers and on the streets, many fans called for the young duo from Santos, Neymar and Ganso, to be included in the squad that would represent Brazil during the World Cup tournament in South Africa.

Neymar drives for the goal in his first match with the national team, August 2010. He scored one of the team's two goals to lead Brazil past the United States.

Obstacles

PELÉ WON HIS FIRST WORLD CUP AT AGE 17. During that 1958 tournament in Sweden, the "king of soccer" was not the star, although he was an important member of the squad that gave Brazil its first World Cup title. In 1994, 17-year-old Ronaldo Nazário de Lima was on the Brazilian squad that won the World Cup in the United States, although the Phenomenon did not play. There was no reason that Brazilian coach Dunga could not call Neymar to the national team for the 2010 World Cup in South Africa.

However, when the final 23-player team was selected, the only Santos player on the list was the veteran Robinho. Dunga preferred to stay with the players that he had worked with during the four years he managed the national team. This frustrated many Brazilians, including former World Cup stars Pelé and Romário, who wanted to see Neymar dribbling and scoring in Africa.

That's not to say that everyone in Brazil wanted to see Neymar on the national team. The World Cup is a very serious matter in Brazil, so there was a percentage of fans who were reluctant to select Neymar, since the young player had never even been capped with Brazil's senior team.

As it turned out, Dunga's selections displeased everyone in Brazil. The team

Brazilian manager Dunga was criticized for not calling Neymar to the 2010 World Cup squad. He was fired after Brazil's disappointing loss to the Netherlands.

did not have a particularly good World Cup tournament. It ended up falling in the quarterfinals against Holland.

First São Paulo, Now Brazil

Neymar would soon show that he was among the best players in Brazil. Soon after the World Cup ended, Santos played for its second championship of 2010. This time it was in a national tournament, the Brazil Cup. The title would qualify Santos for the Copa Libertadores, the most important club competition in South America.

In the first game of the finals, Neymar scored the first goal in the 2-0 victory over Vitória. It was a wonderful performance, with a single flaw—he missed a penalty kick. Neymar had tried to use a strategy known in Brazil as "Cavadinha," This is a soft shot intended to deceive the goalkeeper and drop into the goal. This time the trick didn't work, and the ball just went directly into the hands of the goalkeeper. Some fans criticized Neymar for his boldness, but others defended him. One was his coach, Dorival Júnior, who said after the game, "There was no negligence. It's very simple, when you make the goal is irreverence, when you lose is irresponsibility. Here in Santos we have the gift of irreverence, and it will remain so."

A few days later, Santos lost the second leg of the finals, 2-1. However, on points the team won the Brazil Cup for the first time in its history.

National Team Cap

After the World Cup disappointment in South Africa, Ricardo Teixeira, chairman of the Brazilian Soccer Confederation, decided to reorganize the national team. Teixeira said that he wanted a "rescue of the art of playing football," perhaps in response to the pragmatism Dunga had set for the squad in his four years coaching the team. Famed coach Muricy Ramalho was initially offered the head coaching position. However, he declined, so Mano Menezes—at the time coach of the Brazilian club Corinthians—accepted the challenge.

Neymar of Santos races for the goal during a Copa Libertadores match against Tachira of Venezuela, February 2011.

Preparing for his first game, against the United States, Mano called both Neymar and Ganso to the squad for the first time. The debut of the aces from Santos ended as a 2-0 victory for Brazil, with a goal from Neymar and great performances by both the young striker and his friend Ganso.

The next game would be against Brazil's biggest rival, Argentina. The Argentine team included Lionel Messi, the best player in the world. It was a close game, but Brazil lost 1-0 on a beautiful goal by Messi.

However, some fans began to compare Neymar to Messi, and European clubs started to watch the young player more carefully.

Months of Turbulence

The second half of 2010, however, did not bring good news for Neymar. His close friend Ganso suffered a serious knee injury and needed an operation. Without him, the Santos attack faltered and the team finished below expectations in the Brazilian

Neymar celebrates his first goal for the Brazilian national team, against the United States, on August 10, 2010.

championship. It seemed that the magic days were over.

For Neymar, the worst moment came on September 15, during Santos's 4-2 victory over Atletico-GO. At the 84th minute, when the game was 3-2, Santos was awarded a penalty kick. Dorival Júnior decided that his team's striker Marcel, not Neymar, should take the penalty shot. This decision angered Neymar deeply. He began to stall, keeping the ball at his feet and refusing to pass it, while the coach was on the verge of despair outside the field. When the game finished, both argued severely while going back to the locker room. "What you are doing is not a man's attitude, you're being a punk," said the coach. "I've always protected you, you should not offend me."

The manager of the opposing team was the experienced Rene Simões, who was responsible for Jamaica's qualification for its only World Cup. After the match, Simões gave an interview criticizing Neymar and Santos. A few days earlier, the club had accused opponents of unfairly attacking its star player on the field.

"What this guy has done is unacceptable," said Simoes. "Something must be done. Neymar must be educated soon. If things continue this way, he'll turn into a monster. I told Dorival that he was right to blame him. Neymar today is neither a man nor a great player, he is a project on both fronts. I am disappointed with soccer after this episode."

Despite all the criticism of Neymar's bad behavior, the board of Santos protected the young star. A week after the match against Atletico-GO, Dorival announced that he would not start Neymar in the game against Corinthians. The board responded by firing Dorival.

National team manager Mano Menezes agreed with the criticism of Neymar over this episode. He left the young player out of the last game played by the Brazilian national team in 2010.

The Conquest of America

THE COPA LIBERTADORES IS PROBABLY THE HARDEST competition in world soccer. It features small stadiums in which the opposing fans are just a few feet away from the field, high altitudes, poorly maintained fields, and competition by powerful clubs. Winning is not easy, as only the best teams are able to come out on top. Before Neymar began playing at Santos, for example, the famed Brazilian club had only won the Copa Libertadores when it featured the great Pelé on the squad.

For these reasons the board of Santos prepared the team carefully to fight for the Copa Libertadores in 2011. They hired good reinforcements, such as the midfielder Elano, who had played for Brazil in the 2010 World Cup. They also spared the team at the end of 2010, when it was apparent that Santos could not win the Brazilian title. Above all, the board and supporters of Santos trusted in the talent of their young striker, Neymar, to bring the team victory.

In early 2011 all the spotlights were pointed at Neymar. Despite his off-field problems, such as the fight with Dorival Júnior and the unexpected pregnancy of a girlfriend, Neymar was able to concentrate when on the field. He moved past these obstacles as easily as he passed through his adversaries.

Neymar was so popular that at the end of 2010, a survey made by a sport marketing agency of more than 8,000 Brazilians found that he was the country's most beloved active player. He received almost 13 percent of public preference.

Taking Responsibility

The year 2011 began with a more mature Neymar, both on and off the field. With Paulo Henrique Ganso still recovering from injuries, Santos would need its jewel to shine more than ever if the club wished to revive the Pelé era and recapture the Copa Libertadores. Neymar took the responsibility and started to lead the team. Showing confidence in the player, Mano Menezes called him to play for the national team in a friendly against Scotland in January 2011.

Neymar played very well in his return to the national team. He scored both of Brazil's goals in the 2-0 victory. The magnificent performance was a demonstration of the kind of play Neymar hopes to become known for in his international career. "From the first time I was called, in the game with the United States, I have the

Santos coach Muricy Ramalho gives instructions to Neymar.

thought of making history with the Brazilian national team," he said.

Despite his great performance, Neymar ended up involved in a controversy, even though it was indirect. During the game, a banana was thrown on the field. Some people felt it was a sign of racism directed at the soccer star. Others, including the head of Scottish soccer Hamish Husband, disagreed. "Neymar was booed because we believed he was faking an injury," Husband said. "Racism has no place with us and, if it exists, we intend to get rid of it."

The episode caused some uneasiness among the confederations of the two countries, but was eventually resolved.

America at His Feet

The Copa Libertadores was the primary objective of Santos during the first part of the 2011 season. The season did not begin well, as in its first three matches, the team drew twice and lost another. The club from Vila Belmiro changed its coach and brought

Neymar celebrates after scoring against Peñarol during the Copa Libertadores final at Pacaembu stadium in São Paulo, Brazil, June 2011. Santos defeated the club from Uruguay to win its third Copa Libertadores title.

Fast Fact

In 2011, Neymar had his second disappointment in the Brazilian national team. Despite the expectations of new coach Mano Menezes, Brazil performed poorly in the Copa América, managing to win just one in four games and being eliminated on penalties by Paraguay.

in Muricy Ramalho, who had led Fluminense to the Brazilian title in 2010.

From that point Santos improved and managed to qualify for the Libertadores playoffs with three straight wins. In the first, against Colo-Colo of Chile, Neymar made another great goal, dribbling past three defenders before finishing. However, while celebrating, he took a mask of his face that had been distributed to fans by the sponsor, and ended up receiving a red card. Neymar was widely criticized, although few people understood the rule that caused him to be sent off.

In the last match of group stage, Neymar returned to the team and scored another goal. This time, when he celebrated, he gestured as though he was putting on a mask, to once again silence the critics.

Santos advanced to the knockout stage, where the club eliminated respectively the clubs America from Mexico and Once Caldas from Colombia.

Peñarol, 50 Years Later

In the semifinal, Neymar shone again in two games against Cerro Porteño, a club from Paraguay. Cerro Porteño had edged Santos to finish at the top of their group, and the semifinal game was marked by rough play and flared tempers. The first game was played at Vila Belmiro. Santos won by a score of 1-0. The goal was scored by defender Edu Dracena, after a great play from Neymar. Watching the match, the former Santos star Robinho liked what he saw. "I

Fans of Santos were thrilled when Elano rejoined the team in November 2010. The playmaker is known for his passing and scoring.

Fast Fact

Before Neymar's emergence made Santos a national power again, rival fans used to mock the supporters of the club, calling the Santos fans "widows of Pelé."

was happy to see this play by Neymar," Robinho said. "It was a great goal. "

Santos would play the second game in Asuncion, Paraguay, without Ganso, who had suffered another injury. The club counted on Neymar's talent to keep its hope alive. It ended in a thrilling 3-3 tie, enabling Santos to advance to the final. Neymar scored one of the goals, and his presence made the Cerro Porteño goalkeeper miscommunicate with defender Pedro Benitez. This led to an incredible own goal.

In the finals, Santos would face Peñarol, a powerful Uruguayan club that had won the first Copa Libertadores in 1960. The Peñarol-Santos matchup was one with a lot of history. In 1962, the two teams had also faced each other at the finals of this competition, and Santos, led by Pelé, won.

In the first game of the finals, Neymar once again showed that he was more mature. He came out as team captain because Dracena had been suspended. He was hunted in the field, taking several violent charges, but didn't chicken out and kept breaking through the defense. With Neymar's help, Santos was able to overcome the pressure of the 55,000 voices that filled the Estadio Centenario in Montevideo. The game ended in a scoreless tie.

Reward of a Hero

The decisive match was played at the Pacaembu stadium in São Paulo. Even on a stage in which he was less accustomed to shine, Neymar and his fellows beat Peñarol 2-1, and received their medals from the hands of none other than Pelé.

Neymar's popularity had reached a new height. By ending a period of almost 50 years without Santos winning the Copa Libertadores, the striker became one of the biggest heroes of the history of the club. He was still only 19 years old.

In December 2011 Neymar played in an exhibition with some of the great players of Brazil's history, including Ronaldo, Zetti Zico, Rai, and many players from the national team.

Neymar receives the trophy as "Best Player in America" awarded by the Uruguayan newspaper *El Pais* on January 19, 2012, in Montevideo.

What's Next for Neymar?

NEYMAR HAD WON STATE, NATIONAL, AND CONTINENTAL CLUB championships before he was 20 years old. Now all that was lacking was for the young striker to conquer the world. In early 2011 he would have the opportunity to add an international trophy to his collection, when he was called to play for Brazil in the South American under-20 championship.

For fans of Brazilian soccer, the two major frustrations are the national team's loss to Uruguay in the 1950 World Cup, which Brazil hosted, and the fact that the Brazilian men's soccer team has never won an Olympic gold medal. Because of this second fact, the 2011 South American under-20 championship, held in Peru, held special importance. The top two teams would qualify for places in the 2012 Olympic Games in London, as well as for the 2011 Youth World Cup in Colombia.

Brazil's coach Ney Franco called Neymar and other top young players to the squad. During the competition, Neymar had many highlights. He was the top scorer with nine goals, and was named the most valuable player. Brazil won the tournament for the 11th time, and earned a place at the London Olympics.

After this, the young ace set a new goal: to finally bring an Olympic gold medal back to Brazil with the national team.

A Brazilian Product

Brazil has always been a major exporter of soccer talent. Unable to compete with the wealthiest European clubs, the Brazilians are accustomed to seeing their best players leave the country to shine in the foreign leagues of France, Spain, Italy, England, and other countries. However, in the 2010s the Brazilian economy has grown stronger while the European Union countries were suffering from a financial crisis. This helped to even the financial balance between clubs. Santos seized the opportunity to keep its biggest star.

On November 9, 2011, Luiz Alvaro Oliveira Ribeiro, chairman of Santos, announced the renewal of Neymar's contract. The contract had a clause guaranteeing that Neymar would stay with the club until after the 2014 World Cup tournament, which Brazil would host. Despite offers from major European clubs like Chelsea, Real Madrid, and FC Barcelona, Neymar decided to remain in Brazil for now.

"My goal is not only to be the best player in the world, but also to play in the best championships. And Santos is playing them," the young player explained. "I am very happy here, especially now that I have a son. There is no greater happiness than to have stayed. I intended to be here for a long time, and I'm accomplishing that intention."

In the wake of the agreement between Santos and Neymar, other Brazilian clubs and players made similar decisions. As a result, 2012 marked the first time in many years that more players returned to Brazil than left to play in Europe. This was another sign of Neymar's influence on Brazilian soccer.

Neymarmania

"We now have more than a star, we have a myth," said Santos chairman Ribeiro. "The greatest contribution that Neymar is giving to Santos is the geometric growth of the crowd. It's amazing the phenomenon of passion he arouses among teenagers nationwide. By 2014 we will have the third largest crowd of fans in Brazil, approaching the two largest, and Neymar deserves the credit."

This statement shows how "Neymarmania" took over the country. Both young and old fans talk about the player, and he appears in newspaper ads, magazines, and television. Neymar is still very young, and has not yet reached the peak of his ability. Neymar has grown, overcome challenges, and learned from controversy. Today, he inspires a new generation of kids who dream of being like Neymar. Neymar is one of Brazil's most popular people on Twitter, with 3.2 million followers.

Disappointing Losses

In December 2011, a duel everyone wanted to see occurred in the final match of the FIFA Club World Cup in Japan. Santos and Neymar would met the powerful FC Barcelona team, led by the best player in the world, the Argentine Lionel Messi.

Neymar had scored a great goal in the 3-0 semifinal victory over Kashiwa Reysol of Japan, but the Santos team did not play well against Barcelona. Although they were crushed, 4-0, Neymar received the Bronze Ball as one of the tournament's best players. He also showed maturity in his comments afterward. "The other day I saw an interview with [Barcelona coach] Pep Guardiola, who said that you lose before you can win. Who knows,maybe this can happen with Santos next year."

In July and August of 2012, the teams that had qualified for the Olympic Games began playing their matches in England. The Olympic rules restrict teams to 18 players, and only three of them may be older than 23 years. Neymar joined other young Brazilian stars, such as his friend Ganso, Alexandre Pato, Leandro Damião, and Oscar, on the Olympic team.

Brazil won all three of its matches in the

Fast Fact

Neymar was voted the third best player in the 2011 Club World Cup, behind Lionel Messi and Xavi of FC Barcelona.

group stage and advanced to the knockout round. In the quarterfinals, Brazil defeated Honduras by a 3-2 score, with Neymar scoring the game-winning goal on a penalty kick and also making an assist on a goal by Damião.

In the semifinals, Brazil shut out South Korea, 3-0, to advance to the Olympic finals for the third time in the national team's history.

Brazilian fans had high hopes for the final, but they were sadly disappointed. The Mexican team scored a goal early and another late, and defeated Brazil by a 2-1 score. At the end, Neymar dropped to the ground in despair. "I feel very sad right now," he said after the game.

But the young player did not let the disappointment slow him down. He returned to Brazil with his heart set on helping both Santos and the national team continue to win championships. And knowing Neymar's skills, the club is certainly in a good position to do just that.

FURTHER READING

Bueno, Eduardo. Football: The *Passion of Brazil*. New York: Leya, 2011.

Geringher, Max. *Almanac of the World Cup*. São Paulo: Editora Globo, 2010.

Leite, Milton. *The Top 11 Brazilian Players*. São Paulo: Editora Contexto, 2010.

Máximo, João, and Marcos De Castro. *The Brazilian Football Giants*. New York: Brazilian Civilization, 2011.

Nassar, Luciano Ubiraja. *The Best Football Players of Brazil*. New York: Expression and Art Publishing House, 2010.

INTERNET RESOURCES

www.istoedinheiro.com.br

Site of a major business and news magazine from Brazil.

www.veja.com.br

Site of the principal sports publication in Brasil.

http://esporte.uol.com.br/futebol/biografias/511/ronaldo/

Site of a major sports television channel in Brazil.

www.fifa.com

Official web site of the Fédération Internationale de Football Association (FIFA), the international governing body of futbol (soccer).

INDEX